52-WEEK

DEVOTIONAL

FOR

TEEN BOYS

Published by Midsummer Bloom Books

First Edition: September 2025
Printed in the United States of America

Contents

How to Use This Book

Hey! I'm glad you're here. This book is your weekly guide to grow stronger in faith, character, and confidence—one week at a time. It's written for real life: homework and sports, group chats and late-night thoughts, wins and losses. Every week gives you God's truth, a short and relatable devotional, a prayer you can make your own, a practical challenge, and a moment to reflect. You'll see Scripture quoted from the ESV (English Standard Version) to keep things accurate and clear.

Here's how to make the most of it:

> » Pick one week and stick with it for seven days.

> » Start by reading the verse—slowly. Maybe read it out loud.

> » Read the devotional thought and let it connect to your life.

> » Pray the prayer. Change the words if you need to—it's your conversation with God.

> » Do the challenge. Small steps add up.

> » Use "Take a Moment" to journal, think, or talk with someone you trust.

You don't have to be perfect. You don't have to feel spiritual 24/7. Just show up. God meets you in real life, not just in church. He cares about your group projects, your goals, your team tryouts, your friendships, and your future. He's not asking you to be someone else—He's inviting you to become fully you in Christ.

Ready? Let's go—52 weeks of becoming who God made you to be.

Week 1: Your True Identity

"Therefore, if anyone is in Christ, he is a new creation. The old has passed away; behold, the new has come." — 2 Corinthians 5:17 (ESV)

Devotional Thought

Labels stick. Maybe people see you as the quiet kid, the funny one, the athlete, the smart one, or the kid who made that one mistake. Sometimes we slap labels on ourselves—"awkward," "not good enough," "behind." But God has a different label for you: new creation. In Christ, your identity isn't based on your performance, your past, your stats, or your feed. It's based on what Jesus has done for you.

Being a "new creation" doesn't mean you wake up with a different face or instantly perfect habits. It means the core of who you are has been changed. God has given you a new heart, new desires, and a new direction. It's like getting a new operating system. Your old OS—the one that ran on fear, pride, and trying to impress everyone—is no longer the boss. You may still feel the old notifications buzzing, but you don't have to click them anymore.

Think about a jersey. When you switch teams, you wear new colors and play for a new coach. In Christ, you're on God's team. That means your worth doesn't rise and fall with your wins or losses. You play hard because you're loved, not to get loved. You mess up, and you get back up. You learn. You grow. The old life doesn't get to define your new future.

So the next time a label tries to stick—remember what God says. You are new. You are forgiven. You are His.

A Prayer for You

Father, thank You that in Jesus I am a new creation. Help me let go of old labels and live from the identity You've given me. When I feel pulled back into old patterns, remind me that the old has passed away and the new has come. Teach me to walk in Your truth today. Amen.

Your Challenge

Write "NEW CREATION" somewhere you'll see it—phone lock screen, notebook cover, or mirror. Every time you see it, take five seconds to breathe and say, "In Christ, I am new." Then make one small choice that lines up with your new identity—send the encouraging text, start the homework, walk away from the gossip, or own a mistake and make it right.

Take a Moment

» What label am I ready to let go of?

» What new identity truth do I need to repeat this week?

» One area I want to live "new" in is: _____

Week 2: Finding Strength in Tough Times

"for God gave us a spirit not of fear but of power and love and self-control." — 2 Timothy 1:7 (ESV)

Devotional Thought

Tough times can feel overwhelming—whether it's the pressure of a big game, failing a test, feeling left out, or dealing with uncertainty about the future. Challenges can make you want to freeze, hide, or give up. But here's the truth: God didn't design you to be ruled by fear or hardship. He gave you tools—power, love, and self-control—to face difficulties head-on.

Power means you're not helpless. The Holy Spirit, the same power that raised Jesus from the dead, lives in you. That doesn't mean you won't feel nervous or unsure, but it means you can take the next step with confidence, knowing God is with you. Love means you're secure in God's unconditional care. When you realize God's love is bigger than any situation, you stop needing to prove yourself. Love drives out fear and allows you to act with kindness and courage, even in tough moments. Self-control means you can pause, focus, and choose how to respond. You're not a prisoner to your emotions or circumstances—you can pray, pause, and proceed with wisdom.

Think of a rock climber facing a steep wall. Their heart might race, their hands might sweat, but they take one step at a time, trusting their gear and training. Faith works the same way: it doesn't eliminate challenges, but it gives you the strength to climb higher. Today, when you face tough times, lean on God's power, love, and self-control—and take one courageous step forward.

A Prayer for You

Lord, thank You for giving me a spirit of power, love, and self-control. Help me to lean on You when life feels overwhelming. Give me courage to face challenges with faith and wisdom. Amen.

Your Challenge

Think about one tough situation you're facing right now. Break it into one small, manageable step, and commit to taking that step this week. Before you act, pray: "God, give me strength to move forward."

Take a Moment

» What challenge feels overwhelming to me right now?

» What's one small step I can take to move forward?

» How can I remind myself of God's power when I feel stuck?

Week 3: Friends Who Shape You

"Whoever walks with the wise becomes wise, but the companion of fools will suffer harm." — Proverbs 13:20 (ESV)

Devotional Thought

Your crew matters. The people you spend time with shape your humor, your habits, your language, and your goals—often without you noticing. Proverbs is clear: walk with the wise, and you'll get wiser. Walk with people who don't care about wisdom, and you'll feel the fallout.

This doesn't mean you ditch anyone who isn't perfect. It means you pay attention to direction. Where are your friends headed? Do they challenge you to be better, or do they pull you toward choices you regret? Are you more yourself around them or less? Wise friends don't have it all together, but they're honest, humble, and hungry to grow. They apologize. They show up. They tell you what you need to hear, not just what you want to hear.

Becoming wise isn't just about picking good friends—it's also about being one. Show up on time. Tell the truth. Keep confidences. Celebrate your friends' wins without getting jealous. Pray for them. Invite them into good things. When you become the kind of friend you're looking for, you tend to attract the same.

If your current circle pushes you toward stuff that doesn't honor God, you don't have to make a dramatic announcement. Start making wiser choices, set boundaries, and invest more time with people headed toward Jesus. Your steps set your path; your path shapes your life.

A Prayer for You

God, thank You for the people in my life. Give me wisdom to choose friends who help me grow, and make me a friend who lifts others up. Help me set healthy boundaries and love people well. Amen.

Your Challenge

Audit your circle. List your five closest influences (friends, accounts, creators). Put a "+" if they push you toward wise choices and a "−" if they pull you away. This week, spend extra time with at least one "+" and reduce time with one "−."

Take a Moment

» A wise quality I value in a friend is: _____

» One way I can be a better friend this week:

» Someone I need to thank or encourage:

Week 4: Your Mind and Your Feed

"Finally, brothers, whatever is true, whatever is honorable, whatever is just, whatever is pure, whatever is lovely, whatever is commendable, if there is any excellence, if there is anything worthy of praise, think about these things." — Philippians 4:8 (ESV)

Devotional Thought

Your mind is like a playlist—it shapes your mood and your moves. What you watch, scroll, listen to, and laugh at builds a mental soundtrack. Paul isn't saying "never have fun"; he's giving you a filter: true, honorable, just, pure, lovely, commendable, excellent, praiseworthy. If it doesn't pass the filter, don't let it loop on repeat.

This isn't about legalism or being scared of culture. It's about training your taste to love what gives life. If your feed constantly serves anger, comparison, or trash, your thoughts will tilt that direction. But when you choose content that fuels faith, creativity, and kindness, your inner world gets stronger. You become harder to shake.

Try this: next time you're scrolling and feel worse, ask why. Is it comparison? Fear? Temptation? Then choose to swipe away and reset with something better—Scripture, a message from a trusted pastor, a clean playlist, or a creative hobby.

Your attention is valuable; spend it on what shapes you into who you want to be.

You don't have to be perfect, but you can be intentional. Guarding your mind isn't about avoiding the world; it's about renewing your mind so you can live like Jesus in the world.

A Prayer for You

Lord, help me set a wise filter over my mind. Teach me to think on what is true and lovely. Give me strength to turn away from what drags me down and fill my heart with Your Word. Amen.

Your Challenge

Do a 7-day "feed filter." Unfollow one account that feeds envy, lust, or anger. Follow one account that builds your faith. Add one daily Scripture input (verse of the day, reading plan, or audio Bible) to your routine.

Take a Moment

» What content drains me? Why?

» What content strengthens me? Why?

» One change I'll make to my media habits:

Week 5: Casting Your Cares

"casting all your anxieties on him, because he cares for you." — 1 Peter 5:7 (ESV)

Devotional Thought

Anxiety can feel like a backpack that keeps getting heavier—grades, sports, family stuff, social pressures. Peter doesn't tell you to pretend the backpack doesn't exist. He tells you to cast it on Jesus. Not some of it. All of it. Why? Because He cares for you.

"Cast" is an action word. It's like throwing a heavy bag to someone stronger. You don't have to carry it alone. This is not a one-time toss; it's a daily rhythm. You might pray in the morning and feel the weight lift, then pick it back up by lunch. That's okay. Cast it again. God doesn't get tired of hearing from you.

Sometimes anxiety needs extra help—talking with a counselor, breathing exercises, better sleep, or telling a trusted adult. Those tools aren't a lack of faith; they're wisdom. God uses people and practices to help you. But at the core, peace comes from knowing you are not alone. The One who holds the universe holds you.

So breathe. Remember His care isn't general—it's personal. He sees the due dates and the drama. He's not rolling His eyes at you; He's inviting you closer.

A Prayer for You

Jesus, I cast my anxieties on You because You care for me. Take what I can't carry. Calm my mind and steady my heart. Lead me to wise help and healthy habits, and help me trust You in every situation. Amen.

Your Challenge

Create a "care transfer" habit. Each night, write down three worries. Pray over each one and then draw an arrow to God's name as a sign of casting it on Him. If something's still heavy, tell a trusted adult or mentor.

Take a Moment

» Three current worries I'm casting on God:

» One healthy habit that helps my anxiety:

» Who can I talk to honestly this week?

Week 6: Play Hard, Stay Humble

"Whatever you do, work heartily, as for the Lord and not for men," — Colossians 3:23 (ESV)

Devotional Thought

Whether it's sports, band, gaming, robotics, or chores, effort matters. God doesn't call you to be average—He calls you to give your best. But there's a twist: you're not playing for the crowd, the coach, or the clout. You're playing for the Lord.

When you work "heartily," you bring passion, focus, and discipline. You practice when no one's watching. You learn from mistakes. You listen to feedback. But humility is what keeps your drive from becoming pride. Humility says, "My talent is a gift. My team matters more than my stats. I can celebrate others' wins and own my losses."

Playing for God changes your why. You hustle because He's worthy, not to get noticed. You treat opponents with respect because they're made in God's image. You thank your coaches and parents. You play clean even if others don't. And when you win, you point the glory up. When you lose, you keep your head up and learn.

If you've been coasting, step it up. If you've been chasing applause, aim higher. The Lord sees your effort and uses it to shape your character.

A Prayer for You

God, thank You for the abilities You've given me. Help me work with a full heart and a humble spirit. Keep my focus on You, not on approval. Teach me to be a great teammate and to honor You in every practice and game. Amen.

Your Challenge

Before each practice, assignment, or shift, whisper, "For You, Lord." Afterward, write one sentence about what you learned and one way to improve. Thank someone who helped you.

Take a Moment

» Where have I been coasting?

» What does humility look like on my team?

» One way I can honor God in competition this week:

Week 7: Respect in Every Relationship

"Do to others as you would have them do to you." — Luke 6:31 (NIV)

Devotional Thought

Respect isn't just about being polite; it's about seeing others the way God sees them—as people made in His image. Whether it's your parents, siblings, friends, teachers, or even someone you don't get along with, God calls you to treat others with kindness, patience, and honor.

At home, respect looks like listening instead of rolling your eyes, helping out without being asked, or saying "thank you" more often. With friends, it's about being loyal, speaking kindly, and building each other up rather than tearing each other down. At school, respect means honoring your teachers by showing up, paying attention, and putting in your best effort. Even with strangers, respect can mean holding the door open, giving a smile, or choosing not to judge someone based on their appearance.

But respect isn't always easy. Maybe your sibling knows exactly how to push your buttons. Maybe your parents set rules you don't understand, or your friends let you down. Even in tough situations, God calls you to rise above. Respect doesn't mean you have to agree with everyone or let people treat you poorly. It means responding with patience, humility, and grace—even when others don't deserve it.

Why does respect matter? Because how you treat others reflects your relationship with God. When you show respect, you reflect God's love and set an example for others to follow. Respect isn't about losing your voice; it's about choosing to use your voice wisely.

A Prayer for You

Lord, help me show respect in all my relationships. Teach me to listen, to speak kindly, and to act with patience and love. When things are hard, give me wisdom to respond in a way that honors You. Amen.

Your Challenge

This week, practice respect in three ways:

» At home: Do one act of service each day (like taking out the trash, doing the dishes, or helping a sibling) without being asked.

» With friends: Say something encouraging to someone who needs it.

» At school or in public: Be intentional about showing kindness to someone who might feel overlooked.

Take a Moment

» One way I can show respect with my words:

» One way I can show respect with my actions:

» A relationship where I need to practice patience:

Week 8: Integrity When No One Sees

"Whoever walks in integrity walks securely, but he who makes his ways crooked will be found out." — Proverbs 10:9 (ESV)

Devotional Thought

Integrity is doing the right thing when no one's watching: closing a tab you shouldn't be on, giving credit in a group project, telling the truth about a missed assignment, turning in the wallet you found. It's quiet strength. Proverbs says integrity brings security—you don't have to keep track of lies, hide your search history, or worry about getting caught. You can breathe.

Crooked paths look easier at first. Cheat a little. Lie a little. Cover it up. But every shortcut builds a shaky foundation. Eventually, it cracks. Integrity takes longer, but it builds something you can stand on. People trust you. You trust yourself. And God delights in it.

If you've messed up (we all have), integrity starts with honesty. Tell the truth. Take responsibility. Make it right. Confession isn't weakness; it's the doorway to freedom. God's grace isn't a pass to keep doing wrong—it's power to start doing right.

Ask yourself: Who am I when the room is empty? The more your private life and public life match, the more peace you'll have. Walk straight. It's a good way to live.

A Prayer for You

God, make me a person of integrity. Give me courage to tell the truth, to choose what's right, and to make things right when I fail. Thank You for grace that forgives and strength that helps me grow. Amen.

Your Challenge

Pick one integrity area to strengthen this week—schoolwork honesty, media choices, money, or promises. Tell someone your goal. Set one daily accountability step (check-in text, screen limit, or study plan).

Take a Moment

» Where am I tempted to take shortcuts?

» Who can hold me accountable with grace?

» One step I'll take to walk securely:

Week 9: The Way of Escape

"No temptation has overtaken you that is not common to man. God is faithful, and he will not let you be tempted beyond your ability, but with the temptation he will also provide the way of escape, that you may be able to endure it." — 1 Corinthians 10:13 (ESV)

Devotional Thought

Temptation isn't unique to you. It's "common to man." That's not meant to downplay your struggle; it's meant to remind you that you're not weird, broken, or alone. Everyone faces pressure—to lie, to shade the truth online, to brag, to hold grudges, to look at things that pull your heart away from God. The key isn't pretending temptation doesn't exist; it's looking for the escape route God promises.

God's faithfulness shows up in three ways: He limits the pressure, He strengthens you, and He provides an exit. Sometimes the exit is obvious: close the app, leave the room, change the music. Sometimes it's internal: pray, quote Scripture, text a friend. Sometimes it's longer-term: build new habits, set filters, get accountability. Escape isn't cowardice; it's wisdom.

Temptation usually shows up when you're hungry, angry, lonely, or tired. That's a good time to pause, breathe, and pray. Ask, "What's my way out right now?" Then take it—even if it means looking uncool. Freedom is better than fake approval.

You won't get this perfect, but you can get stronger. When you fall, run to Jesus, not away. Confess. Receive grace. Try again. You're not fighting alone.

A Prayer for You

Lord, thank You for always providing a way of escape. Open my eyes to see it and give me courage to take it. Strengthen me in the moment of temptation and surround me with wise support. Amen.

Your Challenge

Identify your top two temptation triggers and pre-plan your exits. Write them down: "When I feel ___, I will ___." Share your plan with a trusted mentor or friend.

Take a Moment

» What time of day am I most vulnerable?

» What's one verse I can memorize for my struggle?

» Who will I text when I need an escape route?

Week 10: Words That Build

"Let no corrupting talk come out of your mouths, but only such as is good for building up, as fits the occasion, that it may give grace to those who hear." — Ephesians 4:29 (ESV)

Devotional Thought

Words are power tools. You can build with them, or you can break things fast. Jokes, comments, and posts can either lift the room or suck the life out of it. Paul gives us a simple test: Is this helpful? Is this the right time? Will it give grace?

"Corrupting talk" isn't just cussing. It's sarcasm that cuts, gossip that spreads, rumors that ruin, and "just kidding" insults that leave marks. Building words look different: encouragement, truth, apologies, and words that protect others' reputations.

This isn't about losing your personality or never being funny. It's about using your voice on purpose. Be the guy who speaks life into the locker room, the group chat, and the classroom. Cheer for the kid everyone overlooks. Thank your teacher. Ask good questions. Share the compliment you thought but didn't say. When you mess up (and we all do), own it quickly and make it right.

If you want your words to change, fill your heart with better things. Jesus said our words flow from our hearts. The more you soak in Scripture and walk with wise people, the more your speech will sound like grace.

A Prayer for You

God, set a guard over my mouth. Help my words build, not break. Give me wisdom for the right words at the right time, and courage to apologize when I get it wrong. Fill my heart so my speech gives grace. Amen.

Your Challenge

Practice "3-for-1." For every negative comment you're tempted to say, speak three genuine encouragements this week—to a teammate, sibling, or classmate.

Take a Moment

» What kind of words do I want to be known for?

» Someone I need to apologize to:

» Someone I can encourage today:

Week 11: Greatness That Serves

"For even the Son of Man came not to be served but to serve, and to give his life as a ransom for many." — Mark 10:45 (ESV)

Devotional Thought

In a world obsessed with being noticed, Jesus kneels and serves. That flips everything. If anyone deserved people to serve Him, it was Jesus. But He showed greatness by washing feet, feeding crowds, and giving His life. Real strength bends low to lift others up.

Serving doesn't make you a doormat. It makes you like Jesus. It's not about getting used; it's about being useful. In your world, serving looks like carrying equipment, helping a classmate understand the math, sticking up for someone, or doing chores without being asked. It's giving your skills for someone else's good.

You might think, "If I serve, no one will notice." That's okay. God sees. And serving isn't just about them—it changes you. It breaks selfishness and builds joy. You discover your gifts. You learn leadership. You become trustworthy.

Start small. Ask, "What needs to be done?" Then do it. You don't need a title to lead—just a towel and a willing heart.

A Prayer for You

Jesus, thank You for serving me and giving Your life for me. Make me a servant in my home, school, and team. Show me needs I can meet and give me joy in meeting them. Amen.

Your Challenge

Pick one place to serve this week: your home, school, church, or community. Do a consistent act of service three times (e.g., set up chairs, tutor a friend, clean a shared space). Don't post about it; just do it for God.

Take a Moment

» Where can I bring help right now?

» What gift or skill can I use to serve?

» Who is one person I can quietly bless?

Week 12: Responding with Wisdom and Patience

"Know this, my beloved brothers: let every person be quick to hear, slow to speak, slow to anger; for the anger of man does not produce the righteousness of God." — James 1:19-20 (ESV)

Devotional Thought

We all know what it's like to feel anger bubbling up—when your sibling won't leave you alone, when someone spreads rumors about you, or when your coach criticizes you unfairly. Anger isn't always wrong; even God gets angry at injustice. But the problem is that human anger often explodes for the wrong reasons—like pride, impatience, or hurt feelings—and it rarely leads to anything good.

» James gives us a roadmap for handling anger wisely: listen fast, speak slow, and anger slower. Let's break that down:

» Quick to hear: When emotions are high, listening first shows maturity. It doesn't mean you agree with everything; it means you care about understanding the full picture before reacting.

» Slow to speak: Words carry weight. Slowing down your response gives you time to choose words that build trust rather than tear people down.

» Slow to anger: Anger is like fire—if controlled, it can

help you stand up for what's right. But if it's wild, it destroys relationships and your witness for Christ.

» Think about this: when you let anger control you, it's like handing the steering wheel of your life to someone else. But when you pause, pray, and respond with wisdom, you take back control and let God guide you toward the best outcome.

If you've been quick to snap recently, don't let guilt weigh you down. Own it, apologize, and ask God to help you grow.

A Prayer for You

Lord, thank You for being patient with me when I overreact. Help me to pause before I speak or act. Teach me to listen well, respond thoughtfully, and reflect Your grace in everything I do. Amen.

Your Challenge

Create a "pause plan." When you feel heat rising, do three things: step back (physically if needed), breathe in and out slowly five times, and pray, "Jesus, lead my response." Use it at least twice this week.

Take a Moment

» What situations tend to trigger my frustration or anger?

» How can I practice slowing down and listening before I speak?

» Who do I need to apologize to or reconcile with this week?

Week 13: Built for Good Works

"For we are his workmanship, created in Christ Jesus for good works, which God prepared beforehand, that we should walk in them." —
Ephesians 2:10 (ESV)

Devotional Thought

You're not an accident. You're God's workmanship—His artwork, His project, His masterpiece. He crafted you on purpose, with purpose. In Christ, you're remade to do "good works" that God set up ahead of time. That means your life is packed with meaningful opportunities—big and small.

Purpose isn't just about your future career. It's about today's choices. Good works look like integrity when it's hard, kindness to someone lonely, excellence in your homework, prayer for your friends, creativity used for good, and courage to stand for what's right. You don't have to invent purpose; you discover it by walking with God and stepping into the opportunities He puts in front of you.

If you're unsure what you're good at, pay attention to what energizes you and what others affirm. Do you love solving problems, making people laugh, building things, organizing chaos, or helping younger kids? These are clues. Offer them to God and ask Him to aim them.

You won't do everything, and that's okay. You're not called to be someone else—you're called to be you, fully alive in Jesus.

A Prayer for You

Father, thank You that I am Your workmanship. Show me the good works You've prepared for me this week. Use my gifts for Your glory and others' good. Help me walk in what You've planned. Amen.

Your Challenge

Make a "good works map." Draw three circles: Home, School, Friends. In each, write two specific ways you can serve or lead this week. Do them, and reflect on what you learned.

Take a Moment

» What energizes me?

» What do others say I'm good at?

» One good work I can do today:

Week 14: Prayer That Feels Real

"do not be anxious about anything, but in everything by prayer and supplication with thanksgiving let your requests be made known to God." — Philippians 4:6 (ESV)

Devotional Thought

Prayer isn't a performance. It's a conversation with your Father. You don't need fancy words. You don't have to get the vibe right. You just come—honest, thankful, and specific. Paul says to bring everything to God: stress, hopes, fears, and everyday stuff.

If praying feels awkward, start small. Use the "TSP" plan: Thanks (what you're grateful for), Sorry (confession), Please (requests). Or pray Scripture—turn verses into prayers. Pray while you walk, lift, or ride the bus. Set a two-minute timer and talk to God about what's actually on your mind.

Thanksgiving is huge. Gratitude shifts your focus from what's missing to what God's already given. It opens your heart to peace. And be specific. Don't just pray, "Help me at school." Pray, "Help me focus in math at 10:30. Help me be kind to Jake at lunch."

Prayer won't always feel epic, but it roots you in God's presence. The more you practice, the more natural it becomes. Keep showing up. He's listening.

A Prayer for You

Father, thank You for hearing me. Teach me to pray honestly and consistently. I bring You my worries and my day. Give me a grateful heart and a steady mind as I talk with You. Amen.

Your Challenge

Make a 7-7-7 plan: Pray 7 minutes in the morning, 7 in the afternoon, 7 at night for one week. Use a simple structure (Thanks, Sorry, Please). Track what you notice—answers, peace, or new ideas.

Take a Moment

» Three things I'm thankful for today:

» One area I need to confess:

» Three specific requests for this week:

Week 15: Stand Strong in a Crowd

"Do not be conformed to this world, but be transformed by the renewal of your mind, that by testing you may discern what is the will of God, what is good and acceptable and perfect." — Romans 12:2 (ESV)

Devotional Thought

There's a strong pull to blend in—say what they say, laugh at what they laugh at, agree with whatever's trending. But following Jesus means you won't always fit the mold. Paul says don't be conformed (pressed into a shape by outside pressure); be transformed (changed from the inside out by God).

Transformation starts in your mind—what you believe, value, and think about. As God renews your mind through His Word and Spirit, you'll start recognizing what choices align with His will. You'll develop spiritual instincts: "This is good," "That's not for me," "I should speak up," "I should walk away."

When the crowd moves one way and God calls you another, it can feel lonely. Remember, you're not alone. Jesus walked this path first. Courage grows when you decide ahead of time who you are and what you stand for. Don't wait for the pressure moment to make your first decision—pre-decide your boundaries and convictions now.

Standing strong isn't about being loud or rude. It's about quiet resolve, respectful words, and a life that points to something better. People may not agree, but they'll notice.

A Prayer for You

Lord, renew my mind and transform my life. Give me discernment to know Your will and courage to live it, even when it's unpopular. Help me stand strong with humility and love. Amen.

Your Challenge

Make three pre-decisions: one about your media, one about your speech, and one about your friendships. Write them down as "I will" statements and share them with someone who will keep you accountable.

Take a Moment

- » Where am I tempted to conform?
- » What conviction do I need to clarify?
- » Who can stand with me when it's hard?

Week 16: When You Fail, Rise

"for the righteous falls seven times and rises again, but the wicked stumble in times of calamity." — Proverbs 24:16 (ESV)

Devotional Thought

Missed the shot. Bombed the test. Said something dumb. Got cut from the team. Failure feels like a punch to the gut—and the replay button in your head won't stop. Proverbs doesn't say the righteous never fall. It says they fall... and rise again. That's the difference. Not perfection. Direction.

Failure isn't your identity; it's information. It tells you what to work on next, where to ask for help, and how to grow. Think of your life like a video game: every "You Died" screen teaches you the enemy's pattern so you can try again smarter. The righteous get back up because they trust that God's grace is bigger than their mistakes and His plans don't evaporate after a bad day.

Rising again looks practical: reviewing what went wrong, asking your teacher for feedback, getting extra reps, apologizing when you messed up, and setting a new plan. It looks spiritual too: bringing your disappointment to God and letting Him speak worth over you. Jesus didn't quit on you; you don't have to quit on you either.

Here's the secret: every person you admire has fallen—a lot. The difference is they refused to let failure write the final chapter. Let perseverance have its way. Get up, learn, grow. Repeat.

A Prayer for You

Father, when I fall, help me rise again. Teach me to learn from my mistakes, receive Your grace, and keep moving forward. Give me humility to ask for help and courage to try again. Amen.

Your Challenge

Pick one recent failure. Write three lessons you learned and one concrete step you'll take this week. Tell a mentor or parent your plan and ask them to check in with you.

Take a Moment

» A failure I'm still replaying:

» What it taught me:

» My next step:

Week 17: Rest for the Overloaded

"Come to me, all who labor and are heavy laden, and I will give you rest. Take my yoke upon you, and learn from me, for I am gentle and lowly in heart, and you will find rest for your souls." — Matthew 11:28-29 (ESV)

Devotional Thought

Homework. Practice. Group chat. Family. Chores. You're juggling a lot, and even your "breaks" are noisy. Jesus' invitation cuts through the noise: come to Me, and I will give you rest. Not just sleep (though you need that), but rest for your soul—the deep, quiet kind you can't find by scrolling.

Jesus talks about a "yoke," which was a wooden bar that linked two animals so they could pull together. He's saying, "Link your life with Mine. Let Me set the pace. Learn My rhythm." His pace is different: unhurried, purposeful, present. When you're yoked to Him, you don't have to carry life alone or run at a speed that burns you out.

Rest isn't laziness. It's worship. It says, "God, You're God. I'm not. I'll work hard, then I'll trust You enough to stop." Start by building small rest rhythms: a tech-free 30 minutes before bed, a weekly Sabbath block (even two hours) to be off your phone, go outside, read Scripture, and enjoy your people. Trade doomscrolling for a short walk with prayer. Choose margin over constant rush.

You'll notice something: rest clears your mind, fuels your focus, and softens your heart. You don't just do more—you become more like Jesus.

A Prayer for You

Jesus, I come to You with my heavy load. Teach me Your rhythm. Help me work hard and rest well. Give my soul real rest, and show me where to slow down and trust You. Amen.

Your Challenge

Schedule two "rest anchors" this week: one daily (10-20 minutes of quiet, Bible, and prayer) and one weekly (at least 2 hours of no schoolwork or socials—do life-giving things). Put them on your calendar and protect them.

Take a Moment

» Where am I most hurried?

» One habit stealing my rest:

» One change I'll make this week:

Week 18: Dating with Honor

"For this is the will of God, your sanctification: that you abstain from sexual immorality; that each one of you know how to control his own body in holiness and honor," — 1 Thessalonians 4:3-4 (ESV)

Devotional Thought

Dating can be exciting—and confusing. Culture makes it a game of status, looks, and pushing boundaries. God invites you to a better way: holiness and honor. Holiness means set apart—different because you belong to Jesus. Honor means treating the other person like someone made in God's image, not a trophy or a shortcut to feel valued.

Self-control isn't about saying "no" to joy; it's saying "yes" to a deeper joy later. It looks like clear boundaries before you're in a tempting moment: when you hang out, where you hang out, how late it goes, what you watch, and how physical you'll be. Decide in the light so you don't compromise in the dark. Communicate those boundaries with respect—yours and theirs.

Dating with honor also means honesty. Be clear with your intentions. Don't use someone to pass time or boost your ego. Protect hearts—including your own. If things end, be kind and clean. No trash talk. No screenshots. No revenge.

And remember: your worth isn't at the mercy of your relationship status. You are loved by God right now. If you've crossed lines, bring it to Jesus. Confess. Receive grace. Reset. He specializes in fresh starts.

A Prayer for You

Lord, teach me to date with holiness and honor. Give me self-control, wisdom, and respect for others. Guard my heart and mind, and help me reflect Your love in all my relationships. Amen.

Your Challenge

Write five "I will" boundaries for dating/hanging out (time, place, phone use, physical boundaries, accountability). Share them with a trusted mentor. If you're not dating, still make the list—you're training now.

Take a Moment

» What's one boundary I need to clarify?

» Who will keep me accountable?

» How can I show honor this week?

Week 19: Your Digital Footprint

"Keep your heart with all vigilance, for from it flow the springs of life." — Proverbs 4:23 (ESV)

Devotional Thought

Your online life isn't separate from your real life—it's part of your heart's output. What you post, like, watch, and send shapes you. Proverbs says guard your heart "with all vigilance," because your whole life flows from there. That includes your DMs and your For You page.

Guarding your heart online means asking better questions:

» Is this true?

» Will this help me love God and people?

» Will I be glad this is attached to my name a year from now?

Remember: the internet never forgets. Colleges, teams, and jobs check digital footprints. More importantly, your future self will live with your choices. Set wise filters. Use screen time limits. Keep your phone out of your room at night. Curate your follows. If an account constantly feeds anger, lust, or envy—unfollow. Replace it with voices that build faith, creativity, and joy.

Also, be the same person online and offline. No fake tough guy, no anonymous cruelty. Speak life. Respect privacy. Don't forward someone's pain for laughs. When you mess up, delete, confess, and do better.

Your phone is a tool. It'll either train your heart or trash it. Choose training.

A Prayer for You

God, help me guard my heart online. Give me wisdom about what I watch, post, and follow. Make my digital life honor You, and give me courage to change habits that don't. Amen.

Your Challenge

Do a 24-hour "digital audit." Delete three apps or follows that drag you down. Add one Bible input (audio Bible, verse widget) and set your phone to grayscale for one hour a day to reduce doomscrolling.

Take a Moment

» One habit online I need to change:

» One account I should unfollow:

» One account I should add:

Week 20: Be an Upstander

"Open your mouth for the mute, for the rights of all who are destitute. Open your mouth, judge righteously, defend the rights of the poor and needy." — Proverbs 31:8-9 (ESV)

Devotional Thought

You've seen it: someone gets roasted in the group chat, shoved in the hallway, or quietly excluded. It's easy to think, "At least it's not me," and stay silent. Wisdom calls you higher: open your mouth, judge righteously, defend. In other words, be an upstander, not a bystander.

Being an upstander doesn't mean jumping into every conflict like a superhero. It means using your influence to protect and include. That could look like shutting down a cruel joke with, "Not cool." It could be taking a screenshot and reporting harassment to a trusted adult. It could be inviting the lonely kid into your lunch table or group. It's choosing not to forward humiliating videos. It's backing up a victim with your presence: stand next to them, walk with them, listen.

Yes, it can feel risky. But courage grows with practice. And you won't do it alone—ask God for boldness and wisdom. Start small, stay consistent, and bring others with you. When more of us stand up, the culture shifts.

Remember, Jesus stood up for us when we were powerless. When you defend others, you reflect His heart.

A Prayer for You

Lord, make me brave and wise. Help me open my mouth for those who can't, and use my influence to protect and include. Show me when to speak, when to get help, and how to love well. Amen.

Your Challenge

Create a simple phrase you'll use to disrupt cruelty (e.g., "Hey, we don't do that here."). Use it once this week. Also, invite one person who's often left out to join you in something.

Take a Moment

» Where do I see bullying or exclusion?

» Who needs an ally this week?

» Who can stand with me as I stand up?

Week 21: Confidence, Not Ego

"But he gives more grace. Therefore it says,
"God opposes the proud but gives grace to the
humble."" — James 4:6 (ESV)

Devotional Thought

There's a kind of confidence that's steady and kind. Then there's ego—loud, insecure, always needing to win. God isn't anti-confidence; He's anti-pride. Pride pushes God away and puts you at the center. Humility draws God near because it tells the truth: "I need You."

Humble confidence looks like this: you know your strengths, and you use them to serve—without needing applause. You can celebrate others' wins because their success isn't a threat to your worth. You can take feedback without melting down. You try new things, not to prove you're awesome, but because you're willing to grow.

If you notice ego creeping in (flexing, fishing for compliments, putting others down), pause. Ask, "What am I afraid of?" Usually pride is a mask for fear of being average or unseen. God already sees you. He delights in you. You're free to be strong and gentle at the same time.

Jesus is the model—powerful, yet washing feet. That's greatness. Walk that path.

A Prayer for You

God, give me humble confidence. Expose pride in my heart, and replace it with Your grace. Help me use my gifts to serve, receive correction well, and celebrate others. Amen.

Your Challenge

This week, practice two "quiet wins": do something hard and don't post or brag about it. Also, give two specific compliments to teammates or classmates who did well—no comparisons, just celebration.

Take a Moment

- » Where does ego trip me up?

- » What feedback do I need to receive?

- » One way I can serve with my strengths:

Week 22: First Job, First Fruits

"Honor the Lord with your wealth and with the firstfruits of all your produce; then your barns will be filled with plenty, and your vats will be bursting with wine." — Proverbs 3:9–10 (ESV)

Devotional Thought

Got your first paycheck? Mowed lawns? Sold sneakers online? Money feels powerful—and it is. God doesn't want your cash; He wants your heart. Honoring Him with "firstfruits" means you give to Him first, not last. It's a statement: "God, You're my provider."

A simple plan: Give, Save, Live.

> » Give: Choose a percent off the top (10% is a classic starting point). Support your church and maybe a cause you care about.

> » Save: Put another percent toward short-term goals (gear, car) and long-term (college, emergencies).

> » Live: Enjoy the rest wisely. Budget basics first, then extras.

Generosity breaks greed and builds joy. Saving builds stability. Spending with a plan builds freedom. Track your money for one month—even simple notes in your phone. You'll feel more in control and less stressed.

If your budget's tight, start small and be consistent. God honors the heart, not the amount. And be honest—no fudging hours, no "borrowing" from the till, no scamming online. Integrity with money is worship.

A Prayer for You

Father, everything I have comes from You. Teach me to honor You with my money. Make me generous, wise, and content. Provide for my needs and guide my plans. Amen.

Your Challenge

Make a 10–20–70 plan for one month: 10% give, 20% save, 70% live—or choose your own percentages. Track every dollar. At the end of the month, reflect on what changed.

Take a Moment

- » My giving percentage:
- » My savings goal:
- » One spending habit to adjust:

Week 23: Strong Body, Strong Spirit

"Or do you not know that your body is a temple of the Holy Spirit within you, whom you have from God? You are not your own, for you were bought with a price. So glorify God in your body." — 1 Corinthians 6:19-20 (ESV)

Devotional Thought

God cares about your body. Not because He wants you to chase perfect abs, but because your body is where you live and where the Holy Spirit lives in you. You were bought with a price—Jesus' blood—so your body matters.

Glorifying God in your body looks practical:

» Sleep: Aim for 7-9 hours. It's not lazy—it's fuel.

» Nutrition: Real food most of the time. Hydrate. Don't make energy drinks your personality.

» Movement: Train with purpose. Mix strength, cardio, and mobility. Rest days are part of training.

» Purity: Guard what you look at and what you do. Your body isn't a toy; it's a temple.

» Recovery: Stretch, breathe, and manage stress. Your nervous system needs care.

Fitness can become an idol or a tool. Keep it a tool. Don't obsess over the mirror or the scale. Chase strength, health, and longevity, not just aesthetics. Celebrate what your body can do, not just how it looks. Encourage teammates rather than comparing.

And if you've misused your body—through neglect or sin—grace is real. Start fresh today. Small, consistent decisions will change your life.

A Prayer for You

God, thank You for my body. Help me honor You with my habits—sleep, food, exercise, and purity. Fill me with Your Spirit and give me discipline and balance. Amen.

Your Challenge

Choose two habits to lock in for 14 days: a bedtime and a daily movement goal (e.g., 30-minute walk/lift). Track them. Also, set one boundary for purity (filter, accountability, or phone out of room at night).

Take a Moment

» One health habit I need most:

» One boundary I'll set for purity:

» How I'll move my body today:

Week 24: Beat Procrastination

"Go to the ant, O sluggard; consider her ways, and be wise. Without having any chief, officer, or ruler, she prepares her bread in summer and gathers her food in harvest." — Proverbs 6:6-8 (ESV)

Devotional Thought

Procrastination whispers, "Later." Later becomes midnight. Midnight becomes stress. The ant doesn't wait for a reminder or a mood. She starts and stays steady. Wisdom says do the small things now so the big things don't crush you later.

Here's a simple system:

» Break it down: Turn "study for history" into "make 10 flashcards" or "read pages 20–30."

» Start tiny: Promise yourself five minutes. Momentum often shows up after you start.

» Block distractions: Put your phone in another room or use a focus app. Music without lyrics can help.

» Set sprints: Work 25 minutes, break 5. Repeat.

» Reward wisely: After two sprints, take a real break—walk, snack, stretch.

Spiritually, procrastination can creep into your walk with God too—"I'll read later," "I'll pray tomorrow." Start small and steady. Five minutes in the Word consistently beats an hour once a month.

When you finish something early, you feel the quiet confidence of the ant: prepared, not panicked. That's a great way to live.

A Prayer for You

Lord, teach me diligence. Help me start, focus, and finish well. Give me wisdom to plan my time and strength to follow through. Thank You for the peace that comes with steady work. Amen.

Your Challenge

Pick one assignment you've been avoiding. Break it into three steps. Do the first step today. Text a friend a photo of your progress and ask them to check in tomorrow.

Take a Moment

- » My biggest procrastination trap:
- » One tool that helps me focus:
- » What I'll start in the next 24 hours:

Week 25: Share Your Hope

"but in your hearts honor Christ the Lord as holy, always being prepared to make a defense to anyone who asks you for a reason for the hope that is in you; yet do it with gentleness and respect," — 1 Peter 3:15 (ESV)

Devotional Thought

Sharing your faith can feel scary—what if they think I'm weird or ask questions I can't answer? Peter gives a simple play: set Jesus apart in your heart, be ready to explain your hope, and do it with gentleness and respect.

You don't have to have a seminary degree. Start with your story: who you were, how Jesus met you, what's changing now. Keep it honest and short. When you don't know an answer, say, "I'm not sure, but I can find out," then actually follow up. People respect humility.

Gentleness matters. You're not trying to win arguments—you're trying to love people. Ask good questions. Listen more than you talk. Look for where God is already at work in their life. Pray before and after conversations: "God, give me the right words and a kind heart."

Also, live in a way that raises questions. Hope is noticeable—peace in stress, kindness in conflict, integrity when you could cheat. When someone asks why you're different, you're ready.

A Prayer for You

Jesus, You are my hope. Give me courage to talk about You with gentleness and respect. Lead me to people who are open, and give me wisdom to listen well and speak truth in love. Amen.

Your Challenge

Write a 60-second version of your story: life before Jesus, how you met Him, and what's changed. Practice it. Pray for one opportunity to share this week and take it.

Take a Moment

» Who am I praying for by name?

» One question I can ask to start a spiritual convo:

» A resource I can share (verse, video, invite):

Week 26: Doubt Isn't the End

"Immediately the father of the child cried out and said, "I believe; help my unbelief!"" — Mark 9:24 (ESV)

Devotional Thought

Doubt shows up at 1 a.m. You wonder: Is God real? Does prayer work? Why is there pain? Doubt can feel like failure, but it isn't. It's an invitation to bring your questions to Jesus. The desperate dad in Mark 9 holds belief and unbelief at the same time—and Jesus meets him there.

Faith isn't pretending you never question. It's choosing to bring your questions into the light. Start by naming them. Then seek answers with humility. Read Scripture. Ask a pastor, parent, or mentor. Watch or read solid resources. Don't just scroll random hot takes; look for trustworthy voices.

Also, doubt often grows in isolation. Join a small group. Talk with friends who are honest and anchored. Keep showing up to church, even when you don't "feel it." Sometimes you need others' faith to carry you for a while.

And keep practicing what you know: pray, serve, worship. Obedience can lead understanding. Over time, your roots grow deeper, not because you avoided hard questions, but because you asked them with Jesus.

A Prayer for You

Lord, I believe; help my unbelief. Meet me in my questions. Guide me to truth, surround me with wise voices, and strengthen my faith as I seek You. Amen.

Your Challenge

Write your top three doubts. For each, find one Scripture and one trusted resource to explore this week. Schedule a conversation with a mature Christian to talk through them.

Take a Moment

» A question I'm afraid to ask:

» Someone safe I can talk to:

» One practice I'll keep even while I doubt:

Week 27: Lead by Example

"Let no one despise you for your youth, but set the believers an example in speech, in conduct, in love, in faith, in purity." — 1 Timothy 4:12 (ESV)

Devotional Thought

You don't need a title to lead. Paul tells a young Timothy to lead by example—in what you say, how you live, how you love, what you believe, and how you stay pure. People are watching. Not in a paranoid way—in a potential way. Your life gives permission for others to rise.

Leadership looks like showing up early, staying late, and doing what needs to be done. It's speaking respectfully to teachers and coaches, even when you disagree. It's being the same person on Friday night that you are on Sunday morning. It's owning mistakes quickly and making them right.

In speech: be clear, kind, and truthful.

In conduct: keep promises and take responsibility.

In love: notice needs and serve.

In faith: pray first and trust God visibly.

In purity: set boundaries that protect your soul.

When people underestimate you because of your age, don't try to impress them—outlast them. Consistency is loud. Keep stacking faithful days, and God will open doors at the right time.

A Prayer for You

God, make me a leader who looks like Jesus. Help my words, actions, love, faith, and purity set an example. Give me consistency and courage to do what's right when it's hard. Amen.

Your Challenge

Pick one area from 1 Timothy 4:12 and set a measurable goal for seven days (e.g., "speech: no gossip; love: one act of service daily"). Track it and ask a friend to join you.

Take a Moment

- » Which area needs the most growth?

- » A leader I admire and why:

- » One commitment I'll make this week:

Week 28: Forgive and Be Free

"Be kind to one another, tenderhearted, forgiving one another, as God in Christ forgave you." — Ephesians 4:32 (ESV)

Devotional Thought

People will hurt you—friends, family, teammates. Forgiveness doesn't say, "It didn't matter." It says, "I refuse to let bitterness be my boss." Paul ties our forgiveness to Jesus'—we forgive because we've been forgiven.

Forgiveness is a process. Start by acknowledging the wound. Name it. Bring it to God. Then choose—sometimes daily—to release the right to pay them back. This doesn't always restore trust immediately. Forgiveness is given; trust is rebuilt over time with proof. If the situation is abusive or unsafe, get help. Forgiveness doesn't mean staying in harm's way.

What if you're the one who hurt someone? Own it without excuses. Say, "I was wrong. I'm sorry. Will you forgive me?" Then change your behavior. Don't demand quick reconciliation—earn it.

Forgiven people become forgiving people. You'll feel lighter. Your prayers will flow freer. Your relationships can heal. The world says "cancel." Jesus says "forgive." That's power.

A Prayer for You

Jesus, thank You for forgiving me. Help me forgive those who've hurt me and seek forgiveness where I've hurt others. Heal my heart, and teach me to live with kindness and courage. Amen.

Your Challenge

Write a forgiveness letter you may or may not send. Be honest and specific. Pray over it and ask God for your next step—conversation, boundary, or simply releasing it to Him.

Take a Moment

» Who do I need to forgive?

» Who do I need to ask forgiveness from?

» One boundary I need for wisdom:

Week 29: Gaming in Control

""All things are lawful for me," but not all things are helpful. "All things are lawful for me," but I will not be dominated by anything." — 1 Corinthians 6:12 (ESV)

Devotional Thought

Gaming can be awesome—teamwork, strategy, fun with friends. But anything good can take over if we let it. Paul says freedom isn't doing whatever you want; it's not being dominated by anything.

Ask honest questions:

> » Is gaming helping or hurting my grades, sleep, or relationships?

> » Am I more patient or more angry after I play?

> » Do I cancel plans or skip responsibilities to grind?

If you're in control, great—keep it healthy. If the game is in control, make a change. Set limits: play after homework, cap your time, keep your console out of your bedroom, or take a weekly offline day. Communicate with your squad so they know your boundaries. Replace late-night marathons with earlier sessions and real rest.

Use gaming for good—build friendships, be positive in chat, refuse toxic trash talk, and step away when a lobby gets ugly.

Be known as the teammate who brings calm and strategy, not rage.

Remember, you're more than your rank. Your identity isn't tied to your K/D. Keep what's fun in its place.

A Prayer for You

God, thank You for good fun. Help me enjoy games without being dominated by them. Give me wisdom to set limits and strength to keep them. Make me a positive presence online. Amen.

Your Challenge

Set a two-week gaming plan: max daily time, no-play times (e.g., before school), and one offline day. Tell your friends. Evaluate how it affects your mood, sleep, and grades.

Take a Moment

» My current gaming limit (if any):

» One sign gaming is too much:

» One boundary I'll set today:

Week 30: Gratitude on Repeat

"Rejoice always, pray without ceasing, give thanks in all circumstances; for this is the will of God in Christ Jesus for you." — 1 Thessalonians 5:16-18 (ESV)

Devotional Thought

Gratitude isn't pretending life is perfect. It's choosing to notice what's good even when life is messy. Paul says to rejoice always, pray constantly, and give thanks in all circumstances—not for all circumstances. Gratitude shifts your focus from what's missing to what God is doing.

Science even backs this up: thankful people sleep better, stress less, and connect more. Spiritually, gratitude opens your heart to God's presence. When you thank Him for specific gifts—breath in your lungs, a friend who texts back, a sunset after practice—you start seeing Him everywhere.

Complaining is easy. The world trains us to find flaws. Gratitude takes training too. Build reps:

» Start and end your day by naming three things you're grateful for.

» Text someone a thank-you every day.

» Turn complaints into prayers: "God, this is hard, but thank You for __."

Watch what happens. Joy grows. Cynicism shrinks. You become the kind of guy people want on their team—hopeful, steady, real.

A Prayer for You

Father, thank You for Your goodness in my life. Teach me to rejoice, pray, and give thanks in all circumstances. Open my eyes to Your gifts and make me a source of joy to others. Amen.

Your Challenge

Start a 7-day gratitude streak. Each day, write three specific thanks (no repeats) and send one thank-you text. If you miss a day, don't quit—start the streak again.

Take a Moment

» Three things I'm thankful for right now:

» One person I need to thank:

» A hard situation where I can still find gratitude:

Week 31: Pressure at the Party

"My son, if sinners entice you, do not consent."
— Proverbs 1:10 (ESV)

Devotional Thought

You get the invite. The group chat is hyped. Someone hints there'll be stuff there—vapes, alcohol, maybe more. You don't want to be "that guy," but you also don't want to compromise. Proverbs keeps it simple: if they entice you, don't consent. You're not weak for saying no—you're wise.

Peer pressure is sneaky. It doesn't always sound like, "Do this or else." It can be a casual, "Come on, just try it," or a joke at your expense. Decide your line before you get there. Pre-decide what you'll do if someone hands you a drink, offers you a hit, or wants you to go somewhere sketchy. Plan your words. Plan your exit. It's way easier to stick to a plan than to invent one in the moment.

Also, bring allies. Tell a trusted friend you're committed to staying clean and ask them to stand with you. If you do go to hang out, keep your ride independent so you can leave when you need to. And remember: you can always skip the scene. There are better ways to spend a Friday night than making choices you'll regret Saturday morning.

You're not missing out on anything that builds real life. Courage now protects your future. God isn't trying to ruin your fun—He's guarding your freedom.

A Prayer for You

Lord, give me strength to say no when I'm pressured to do what's wrong. Help me choose friends and places that honor You. Give me words and a way out when I need it. Amen.

Your Challenge

Write three pre-decisions and memorize them: "If I'm offered __, I will __." Text them to a friend who will back you up. Arrange your own ride for the next hangout.

Take a Moment

» My biggest party pressure:

» My exit line:

» Who will back me up?

Week 32: Honesty at School

"Lying lips are an abomination to the LORD, but those who act faithfully are his delight." —
Proverbs 12:22 (ESV)

Devotional Thought

The temptation is everywhere: copy a friend's homework, sneak a look at your notes, "borrow" a sentence from a site and call it yours. It feels small—until it isn't. God cares about truth not because He's nitpicky, but because truth builds trust. Cheating steals from your character and your future, even if you don't get caught.

Acting faithfully looks like doing your own work, owning mistakes, and asking for help when you're stuck. It's emailing your teacher to clarify an assignment instead of panicking and plagiarizing. It's taking a lower grade rather than lying. That's not weakness—that's integrity. And integrity travels. Teachers, coaches, and future bosses notice it.

If you've crossed a line, don't double down. Tell the truth. Accept the consequence. Make it right. Confession is painful but freeing. You'll sleep better knowing you reset your compass.

Honesty doesn't mean perfection. It means you keep your heart clean and your path straight. God delights in that. And honestly? So will you.

A Prayer for You

God, make me faithful in my work. Give me courage to be honest when it's hard and help me ask for help instead of cutting corners. Build my character for the long run. Amen.

Your Challenge

Pick one class where you're tempted to cheat. Make a plan: teacher office hours, study group, or tutoring. Delete any saved answers or shady sites from your device. Tell one person your commitment.

Take a Moment

- » My biggest honesty temptation:

- » One support I'll add:

- » One step to make things right (if needed):

Week 33: Sibling Strength

*"Love one another with brotherly affection.
Outdo one another in showing honor." —
Romans 12:10 (ESV)*

Devotional Thought

Siblings can be your best teammates and your most annoying opponents—sometimes in the same hour. The daily stuff piles up: borrowed hoodies, noise at the worst time, attitude. Paul's challenge is wild: outdo one another in showing honor. Make it a competition to respect each other.

Honoring your siblings looks like listening, sharing, apologizing quickly, and protecting them in public (even if you clash in private). It means not roasting them in front of friends or exposing their personal stuff online. It's offering help without being asked and celebrating their wins without making it about you.

If there's deep conflict, start small. Pick one habit to change—a kinder tone, a daily check-in, or five minutes helping with chores. Pray for your siblings by name. Ask God to give you His heart for them. You won't feel it every day, but love grows with practice.

Your home is your first training ground. If you can love well there, you can love well anywhere.

A Prayer for You

Father, help me honor my siblings. Give me patience, kindness, and humility. Heal any tension and make our home a place of peace and teamwork. Amen.

Your Challenge

Do a "silent assist" each day: one thing that makes your sibling's life easier (clean their dish, help with homework, share the charger) without announcing it. Also, speak one genuine compliment to them this week.

Take a Moment

» One way I can honor a sibling today:

» One apology I need to make:

» One boundary we should set together:

Week 34: When You Face Loss

"The LORD is near to the brokenhearted and saves the crushed in spirit." — Psalm 34:18 (ESV)

Devotional Thought

Loss hits hard—losing a grandparent, a friend moving away, a pet dying, even a dream falling apart. Grief feels heavy and weird. One day you're okay, the next you're not. God doesn't stand far off; He draws near to the brokenhearted. He doesn't rush you. He holds you.

Give yourself permission to feel. Cry if you need to. Talk to someone you trust. Write what you miss. Look at photos. Tell stories. The goal isn't to "get over it," but to walk through it with God. Jesus wept at His friend's tomb—grief isn't a lack of faith; it's love mourning what was lost.

Pray simple prayers: "God, be near." "Jesus, hold me." Open your Bible to the Psalms and pray those words. Let others serve you—meals, rides, company. Keep the good routines: sleep, food, movement, and being around safe people.

If grief lingers heavy or turns into numbness, tell a counselor or pastor. That's wisdom, not weakness. Healing takes time, and God is patient. He promises to be close, and He keeps His promises.

A Prayer for You

Lord, I'm hurting. Be near to me. Comfort me and carry me when I'm tired. Give me people who will listen and help me take the next step. Heal my heart over time. Amen.

Your Challenge

Create a small remembrance: write a letter, make a playlist of meaningful songs, or plant something in honor of what you lost. Share one memory with someone who understands.

Take a Moment

» What am I grieving?

» Who can I talk to?

» One healthy habit I'll keep this week:

Week 35: Kill the Comparison

"A tranquil heart gives life to the flesh, but envy makes the bones rot." — Proverbs 14:30 (ESV)

Devotional Thought

Comparison is everywhere: someone else's PR, someone else's grades, someone else's relationship, someone else's highlights. It feels like motivation—but it often rots your joy from the inside. God offers a different engine: a tranquil (settled) heart.

A tranquil heart comes from knowing who you are in Christ and running your race, not theirs. It doesn't mean you don't train hard or set goals. It means your worth isn't on the line. You can celebrate others without shrinking and improve yourself without hating yourself.

Practical steps:

» Limit the scroll that triggers envy.

» Name what you admire in someone and turn it into inspiration: "What can I learn?"

» Practice gratitude—three daily specifics.

» Set your own metrics: effort, growth, consistency. Track your progress against yesterday you, not their today.

When envy pops up, pray for the person you're comparing yourself to. Nothing kills envy like blessing. And remind yourself: God has unique plans for you that no algorithm can rank.

A Prayer for You

Father, calm my heart. Free me from envy and teach me contentment. Help me run my race with joy, celebrate others, and grow without comparing. Amen.

Your Challenge

Pick one platform or account that triggers comparison and unfollow or mute it for a week. Replace that time with 10 minutes of working on your own growth (skill practice, reading, training).

Take a Moment

- » Where do I compare most?

- » One person I can genuinely celebrate:

- » My growth metric this month:

Week 36: Mornings That Matter

"O LORD, in the morning you hear my voice; in the morning I prepare a sacrifice for you and watch." — Psalm 5:3 (ESV)

Devotional Thought

Mornings set the tone. Hit snooze five times, rush out the door, and the day chases you. Start with intention, and you lead the day. David says God hears his voice in the morning—he brings something to God and then watches for what God will do.

You don't need a two-hour routine. Try 10–15 minutes:

» Wake up five minutes earlier than usual.

» Drink water, breathe, stretch.

» Open your Bible (start with a Gospel or Proverbs). Read a short passage.

» Pray simply: Thanks, Sorry, Please.

» Preview your day and ask, "God, where can I bring You with me?"

Add small anchors: make your bed, pack your bag the night before, put your phone across the room. Protect your first minutes from notifications—your soul doesn't need the drama at 6:30 a.m.

Night routines help mornings. Set a consistent bedtime. Lay out clothes. Charge your phone outside your room if possible. You'll be shocked how much stronger and calmer you feel when you begin with God.

A Prayer for You

Lord, meet me in the morning. Help me start my day with You—Your Word, Your presence, Your peace. Order my steps and make me attentive to Your voice. Amen.

Your Challenge

Build a 7-day morning routine. Write it down and stick it on your wall. Keep it short and winnable. Track it and adjust after a week.

Take a Moment

» One thing that derails my mornings:

» One anchor I'll add at night:

» A verse I'll read tomorrow:

Week 37: Faith Beyond Sunday

"And let us consider how to stir up one another to love and good works, not neglecting to meet together, as is the habit of some, but encouraging one another..." — Hebrews 10:24-25 (ESV)

Devotional Thought

Faith isn't just about what happens on Sunday morning—it's about how you live every day. But here's the truth: we're not meant to do faith alone. God designed us for community because we grow stronger when we're surrounded by people who encourage us, challenge us, and point us back to Him.

Church is one of the best places to find that kind of community. It's not about ticking a box or sitting in a pew—it's about connecting with others who are also figuring out what it means to follow Jesus. It's where you can ask questions, worship together, and serve others. Think of it like a team: every player has a role, and you're part of God's team.

Even beyond Sunday, faith grows in the little things. It's in the way you treat your classmates on Monday, how you show kindness to your family on Wednesday, and how you pray for someone who's struggling on Friday. Church is a starting point, but your faith is meant to follow you into your week.

What if church hasn't been a good experience for you? Maybe it's felt boring, judgmental, or even hurtful. That matters to God. He loves His church and is committed to healing it.

Look for leaders or groups where you feel safe and seen. And remember, church isn't perfect, but it's full of imperfect people trying to follow a perfect God.

Faith isn't about a building; it's about building a life that reflects God's love every day.

A Prayer for You

Jesus, thank You for giving me a community to grow in faith. Help me see church as more than a Sunday event and guide me to live out my faith every day. Show me how to encourage others, serve with love, and follow You with my whole life. Amen.

Your Challenge

This week, think about how your faith can go beyond Sunday:

» At church: Write down one thing you learned during the service and share it with someone.

» In your week: Do one act of kindness for someone who might need encouragement.

» In your community: Ask a leader, small group, or mentor how you can get involved in serving others.

Take a Moment

» One way I can live out my faith during the week:

» One thing I can do to encourage someone else:

» A way I can make church feel more meaningful for me:

Week 38: Do Justice, Love Mercy

"He has told you, O man, what is good; and what does the LORD require of you but to do justice, and to love kindness, and to walk humbly with your God?" — Micah 6:8 (ESV)

Devotional Thought

The world is messy—unfair rules, prejudice, poverty, people getting overlooked. God cares deeply about justice and kindness, and He invites you to join Him. Not with loud posts and no action, but with humble steps that make a difference.

Do justice: Treat people fairly. Tell the truth. Don't cheat. Stand up for those being pushed out. Use your voice to report wrongs and your time to help make them right. Love mercy (kindness): be generous, forgive quickly, and look for needs you can meet. Walk humbly: remember you don't know everything. Listen to people's stories. Learn before you speak. Pray for wisdom.

Start where you are: your school, neighborhood, team, and online spaces. Tutor a younger student. Volunteer at a local ministry. Join a service project. Be consistent. Justice is less a one-time moment and more a lifestyle of faithful love.

Jesus is your model—full of truth and grace. Follow Him into the hard places with a soft heart.

A Prayer for You

God, show me how to do justice, love kindness, and walk humbly with You. Open my eyes to needs around me and give me courage to act with wisdom and love. Amen.

Your Challenge

Pick one justice/mercy action this month: serve at a food bank, join a tutoring program, or help a classmate who's struggling. Put it on your calendar and invite a friend.

Take a Moment

- » What injustice do I notice most?

- » Who can I learn from?

- » One practical step I'll take:

Week 39: Coachable

"Listen to advice and accept instruction, that you may gain wisdom in the future." —
Proverbs 19:20 (ESV)

Devotional Thought

Being coachable is a superpower. It's not just for sports—teachers, parents, bosses, and mentors are all "coaches" in your life. Coachable guys have three traits: they listen, they apply, and they follow up. They don't get defensive when corrected. They lean in, learn fast, and keep growing.

Next time you get feedback, try this:

> » Breathe and listen fully.

> » Ask clarifying questions: "What's one thing I should change first?"

> » Repeat back what you heard.

> » Thank them.

> » Make a plan and check in later: "Here's what I tried—any tips?"

Humility accelerates growth. Pride stalls it. You don't have to love correction, but you can learn to value it. The sooner you do, the faster you improve in class, on the field, at work, and in life.

God uses human coaches to shape you. Don't waste the wisdom around you.

A Prayer for You

Lord, make me coachable. Give me a humble heart to receive instruction and the grit to apply it. Help me grow through the people You've placed in my life. Amen.

Your Challenge

Identify one person to ask for feedback this week. Ask for one specific area to improve and one drill or practice to do. Do it for seven days and report back.

Take a Moment

» Where am I defensive?

» Who gives me honest feedback?

» One skill I'll work on this week:

Week 40: Care for God's Earth

*"The LORD God took the man and put him in the garden of Eden to work it and keep it." —
Genesis 2:15 (ESV)*

Devotional Thought

From the start, God gave humans a job: work the earth and keep it. Caring for creation isn't political—it's biblical. The world God made is good, and loving Him includes stewarding what He's entrusted to us.

You don't have to be a scientist to make a difference. Start simple:

» Reduce waste: reusable bottle, less single-use plastic.

» Recycle right: learn your local rules.

» Respect spaces: pick up trash at the field, trail, or parking lot.

» Conserve: turn off lights, take reasonable showers, carpool when possible.

» Enjoy creation: hike, fish, garden. People protect what they appreciate.

Creation care shows respect for the Creator and love for your neighbors who share this planet. It also shapes your character—discipline, gratitude, and attention to detail.

Remember, you're not saving the world alone. You're joining God in keeping it.

A Prayer for You

Creator God, thank You for the world You made. Teach me to work it and keep it well. Help me form habits that honor You and bless others. Amen.

Your Challenge

Choose one creation-care habit for 30 days (carry a reusable bottle, bike/walk once a week, or pick up five pieces of trash daily). Invite a friend to join you and track your progress.

Take a Moment

- » One habit I can change today:

- » A place in nature that helps me feel close to God:

- » How I'll enjoy creation this week:

Week 41: What You Sing Shapes You

"Let the word of Christ dwell in you richly... singing psalms and hymns and spiritual songs, with thankfulness in your hearts to God." —
Colossians 3:16 (ESV)

Devotional Thought

Music is powerful. It gets in your head and your heart faster than almost anything. Paul links God's Word and songs—what you sing helps what God says sink deep. This doesn't mean you can only listen to worship, but it does mean your playlist matters.

Ask:

» What messages are these lyrics feeding me?

» Do they pull me toward purity, courage, and gratitude—or away?

» How do I feel after bingeing this artist?

Build a balanced playlist:

» Add worship tracks that point you to Jesus.

» Find clean versions or artists who elevate without trashing your soul.

» Use music as a cue—worship on the way to practice, instrumental for study, hype that isn't hateful for the gym.

Also, sing at church. Even if your voice cracks. Singing truth together forms your heart and strengthens your faith. Thankfulness grows when you put it to melody.

Your ears are a gate. Guard them well—and enjoy music as the gift it is.

A Prayer for You

God, shape my heart through what I hear and sing. Let Your Word dwell in me richly. Help me choose music that builds me up and fills me with gratitude. Amen.

Your Challenge

Curate a "faith + focus" playlist this week: 10 worship songs and 10 clean, uplifting tracks. Use it during your commute or workouts. Remove two songs that pull you the wrong way.

Take a Moment

- » One song that lifts my faith:
- » One song I should cut:
- » When will I use my new playlist?

Week 42: Pray for Your Enemies

"But I say to you, Love your enemies and pray for those who persecute you," — Matthew 5:44 (ESV)

Devotional Thought

There's that guy who talks trash, the teacher you think is unfair, or the ex-friend who turned on you. Jesus' command is shocking: love your enemies and pray for them. Not because what they did was okay, but because love breaks cycles of hate.

Praying for an enemy doesn't mean denying the hurt. It means bringing the hurt to God and asking Him to work in both hearts. Start simple: "God, help them. Help me." Pray for their good—wisdom, peace, healing. Ask God to show you if there's anything you need to own, and to give you wisdom about boundaries.

Loving an enemy looks like refusing revenge, speaking respectfully, and doing good when you have the chance. It doesn't mean staying in harm's way—get help if you're unsafe. But when you're free from the need to get even, you're truly free.

This is hard. It's also powerful. It makes you look like your Father.

A Prayer for You

Father, help me love my enemies. Heal my heart and theirs. Give me wisdom, strength, and the courage to pray and do good. Protect me where I need boundaries, and make me more like You. Amen.

Your Challenge

Write the initials of one "enemy" or difficult person. Pray for them for seven days. If appropriate, do one quiet act of kindness (a respectful message, a favor, or choosing not to clap back).

Take a Moment

- » Who is hard for me to love?
- » What boundary do I need?
- » What can I pray for them?

Week 43: Decisions About Your Future

"Trust in the LORD with all your heart, and do not lean on your own understanding. In all your ways acknowledge him, and he will make straight your paths." — Proverbs 3:5-6 (ESV)

Devotional Thought

College or trade? Which classes? What team? What job? The future can feel like a maze. God doesn't hand you a full map, but He promises direction as you trust Him step by step.

Trust looks practical:

» Pray about decisions, big and small.

» Get counsel from wise people who know you—parents, mentors, teachers.

» Pay attention to your gifts and what energizes you.

» Do the next right thing that's in front of you.

Don't wait for a lightning bolt. Often, God guides through open doors, closed doors, and steady peace as you move. If you're paralyzed by fear of choosing "wrong," relax. God is a Shepherd. He can redirect you. Your job is to stay close and obedient.

Make a simple plan, then hold it with open hands. Work hard where you are, and trust God with where you're going.

A Prayer for You

Lord, I trust You with my future. Give me wisdom, counsel, and courage to take the next right step. Direct my paths and align my plans with Your will. Amen.

Your Challenge

Create a one-page "next steps" plan: top three options for after high school, skills to build, people to ask for input, and deadlines for applications or visits. Schedule two conversations with trusted adults.

Take a Moment

» What energizes me?

» Who will I ask for counsel?

» My next right step:

Week 44: Contentment Over Clout

"Not that I am speaking of being in need, for I have learned in whatever situation I am to be content." — Philippians 4:11 (ESV)

Devotional Thought

There's always a newer phone, a hotter drop, a cleaner build. It's easy to chase clout—stuff that says, "Look at me." Paul learned contentment—a skill, not a personality trait. Contentment says, "I can enjoy what I have, work for what I need, and not be owned by any of it."

Practice contentment:

» Delay one purchase for 30 days. See if you still want it.

» Set a budget and stick to it.

» Celebrate what others have without making it your identity.

» Give generously—generosity breaks greed.

Contentment isn't settling. It's being steady. You can still grind for goals—just don't let the grind grind you up. Your identity isn't in your gear, your follows, or your flex. It's in Jesus, who never goes out of style.

The secret Paul mentions later is Jesus' strength. With Him, you can handle scarcity and abundance without losing your soul.

A Prayer for You

God, teach me contentment. Free me from chasing clout and help me enjoy and steward what I have. Make me generous and grounded in You. Amen.

Your Challenge

Do a "no-buy" week for non-essentials. Track every time you feel the impulse to buy and what triggered it. At week's end, give a small amount to bless someone in need.

Take a Moment

» One thing I'm tempted to chase:

» One budget step I'll take:

» One way I'll practice generosity:

Week 45: Be a Bridge—Invite and Include

"Nathanael said to him, "Can anything good come out of Nazareth?" Philip said to him, "Come and see."" — John 1:46 (ESV)

Devotional Thought

Some friends think church is cringe or Jesus is irrelevant. You don't have to argue them into faith. Be like Philip: "Come and see." Be a bridge between your friends and Jesus—through your life, your invite, and your friendship.

Bridging looks like:

» Pray for your friends by name.

» Live with integrity and kindness that raises questions.

» Invite them to youth group, a game night, or a service project—low-pressure, high-fun.

» Sit with them when they come. Explain stuff. Introduce them to your friends.

» Follow up: "What did you think?" Listen without pushing.

Even if they say no, keep being a solid friend. Sometimes people need to belong before they believe. Your consistent presence is powerful.

Don't forget: you're not the Savior. Jesus is. Your job is to bring people to where He is moving and trust Him with their hearts.

A Prayer for You

Jesus, make me a bridge. Give me courage to invite and the patience to walk with my friends as they explore faith. Use my life and my words to point them to You. Amen.

Your Challenge

Write down three names. Pray daily for them for two weeks. Invite at least one to church or youth group this month. Plan to sit with them and grab food after.

Take a Moment

» Three names I'm praying for:

» What event is best to invite them to?

» How I'll follow up:

Week 46: Money Traps and Wise Wins

"Wealth gained hastily will dwindle, but whoever gathers little by little will increase it."
— Proverbs 13:11 (ESV)

Devotional Thought

Your feed promises fast money: flips with zero risk, "no-loss" sports picks, "guaranteed" crypto gains, paid surveys that want your info, and sketchy DMs about reselling. It's all speed and hype. Proverbs cuts through: money that comes fast usually goes fast. Real growth is "little by little."

That doesn't mean you can't hustle. It means you choose wisdom over hype. Work a real job. Offer legit services (mowing, tutoring, editing). Track your income and expenses. Build skills that outlast trends. Most "secret methods" you see online are someone else's way of making money... off you.

Watch for red flags:

» Pressure to decide now.

» Vague promises, no clear plan.

» Pay upfront to access "insider info."

» No accountability or reviews from real people you trust.

» Anything illegal (sports betting is illegal for minors) or dishonest.

Instead, create a simple money path: Give first (honor God), save second (build stability), and live on the rest (with a plan). Over time, small smart moves beat flashy "wins." You sleep better when your money story is honest.

Remember: God cares more about the person you're becoming than the dollars in your account. Choose slow, steady, and faithful. That's how you win for real.

A Prayer for You

Father, give me wisdom with money. Protect me from scams and shortcuts. Help me work with integrity, give generously, save patiently, and live content. Amen.

Your Challenge

Make a "hype filter" checklist. Before any money decision, answer: Is it legal? Is it honest? Do trusted adults confirm it? Can I explain how it works? If any answer is no, walk away. Also, set a 72-hour rule for non-essential purchases this week.

Take a Moment

» One money trap I've seen:

» One honest way I can earn this month:

» My give/save percentages:

Week 47: Rumors, Receipts, and Respect

"For lack of wood the fire goes out, and where there is no whisperer, quarreling ceases." —
Proverbs 26:20 (ESV)

Devotional Thought

Rumors spread like wildfire—screenshots, half-truths, and "Did you hear...?" It can feel harmless or entertaining, until someone's reputation gets burned. Proverbs says gossip needs fuel. If you stop feeding it, it dies.

Ask yourself:

» Do I hit forward before I check facts?

» Do I laugh at "tea" that would crush me if it were about me?

» Do I talk about people the same way I'd talk to them?

Respect looks like refusing to carry a story you didn't see. It looks like saying, "I don't know if that's true, so I'm not sharing it." It looks like shutting down group-chat pile-ons and not posting subtweets designed to hurt. It's also going to the person directly if you have a problem, not to an audience.

If you've added wood to a fire, own it. "I shared something I shouldn't have. I'm sorry." Delete the post. Tell the people you told that you were wrong. That takes real courage—and it helps heal what was harmed.

Be the guy people trust with their name when they're not in the room. You won't regret it.

A Prayer for You

Lord, set a guard over my mouth and my posts. Help me refuse gossip and be a source of truth and peace. Give me courage to make things right when I mess up. Amen.

Your Challenge

For seven days, be a "firefighter": don't forward unverified content. If gossip starts, say one sentence to stop it ("Let's not." "We don't know the full story."). Then change the subject or walk away.

Take a Moment

» One place gossip spreads fastest in my world:

» A phrase I'll use to shut it down:

» Someone I need to apologize to:

Week 48: When God Feels Silent

"How long, O LORD? Will you forget me forever? How long will you hide your face from me? How long must I take counsel in my soul and have sorrow in my heart all the day?" —
Psalm 13:1-2 (ESV)

Devotional Thought

You've prayed—for a healing, a spot on the team, a friendship to mend, a family situation to change—and nothing seems different. The silence gets loud. Psalm 13 shows you're not alone. David, a man after God's heart, asked, "How long?" He brought his honest pain to God, not polished lines.

Silence doesn't mean absence. Sometimes God is working in ways you can't see yet—building patience, aligning timing, preparing people, shaping your character. Like seeds underground, growth happens before it's visible. Your job isn't to control outcomes; it's to keep coming close.

Try this rhythm:

> » Lament: Tell God exactly how it feels. He can handle it.

> » Look back: Remember past answers and faithfulness—write them down.

> » Live faithful: Keep doing the next right thing—pray, serve, study, train.

» Lean on others: Ask friends, mentors, and your church to pray with you.

» Leave it with Him: End with, "Yet I trust You."

David's psalm starts with "How long?" and ends with "I will sing." The situation didn't instantly change—but his heart did. God met him in the waiting. He'll meet you too.

A Prayer for You

God, when You feel silent, hold me close. Hear my "how long" and strengthen my trust. Help me remember Your faithfulness and keep walking with You while I wait. Amen.

Your Challenge

Start a "faithfulness list." Write 10 times God has come through (big or small). Add one new item each day this week. Read it when discouragement hits.

Take a Moment

» What unanswered prayer weighs on me?

» Who can I ask to pray with me?

» One faithful step I'll take today:

Week 49: Everyday Life with the Holy Spirit

"But the fruit of the Spirit is love, joy, peace, patience, kindness, goodness, faithfulness, gentleness, self-control; against such things there is no law." — Galatians 5:22–23 (ESV)

Devotional Thought

The Holy Spirit isn't a vibe; He's God living in you. He doesn't just show up at camp or worship nights—He's with you on the bus, in math, at practice, and in the group chat. How do you know He's at work? Fruit. Not instant perfection, but growing evidence: love, joy, peace, patience, kindness, goodness, faithfulness, gentleness, self-control.

Think of your heart like soil. You can't force fruit, but you can create conditions for growth:

> » Sunlight (Scripture): Read and reflect on God's Word daily.

> » Water (Prayer): Talk to God honestly throughout your day.

> » Weeding (Repentance): Pull out attitudes and habits that choke growth.

> » Community (Church): Grow with others who follow Jesus.

Invite the Spirit in real-time: "Holy Spirit, help me be patient right now." "Give me self-control on my phone tonight." "Produce kindness in this conversation." Then act on the nudge. The Spirit empowers obedience, and obedience strengthens your sensitivity to Him.

Over time, the fruit shows up where you used to react. You become steadier, kinder, stronger. That's not just self-improvement—that's God at work in you.

A Prayer for You

Holy Spirit, fill me today. Grow Your fruit in my life and make me responsive to Your leading. Help me live like Jesus in my words, thoughts, and actions. Amen.

Your Challenge

Pick one fruit you need most this week. Find one verse about it. Each morning, pray specifically for that fruit, and each night, write one moment you saw it grow.

Take a Moment

» Which fruit is most missing right now?

» What "weed" is choking growth?

» One way I'll create better "soil" today:

Week 50: Eyes Up— Fighting Lust

"Blessed are the pure in heart, for they shall see God." — Matthew 5:8 (ESV)

Devotional Thought

Lust promises quick thrills and leaves you emptier. In a world of constant screens, it's normal to feel this fight. Jesus calls you to purity of heart—not because He's anti-desire, but because He designed desire for real love, not pixels. Purity clears your vision so you can see God and others rightly.

This battle is winnable, but not solo. Start with honesty: confess to God and to a trusted mentor or parent. Shame loses power in the light. Then set smart boundaries:

» Keep devices out of your bedroom at night; charge in a common space.

» Use filters and accountability software with a trusted adult.

» Identify triggers (bored, late, lonely, stressed) and pre-plan alternatives: text a friend, take a walk, do push-ups, read Scripture, go to sleep.

» Curate your feed—unfollow accounts that bait lust.

» Go old-school: memorize verses that strengthen your mind.

When you slip, run to Jesus, not away. Confess quickly, receive grace, and reset. Progress often looks like shorter falls, quicker honesty, and longer stretches of freedom. Celebrate wins and keep going.

Your sexuality is part of God's good design. He's not out to crush you—He's out to free you. Eyes up. Heart pure. Step by step.

A Prayer for You

Jesus, make my heart pure. Forgive me where I've fallen and strengthen me to walk in freedom. Give me wisdom, accountability, and new desires that honor You and others. Amen.

Your Challenge

Create a purity plan: bedtime boundary, filter installed, two trigger replacements, and one accountability person. Share it and schedule a weekly check-in for a month.

Take a Moment

- » My biggest trigger:
- » One account I need to unfollow:
- » Who will I ask to keep me accountable?

Week 51: Time That Tells the Truth

"So teach us to number our days that we may get a heart of wisdom." — Psalm 90:12 (ESV)

Devotional Thought

Your time tells the truth about your priorities. You might say school, faith, family, and training matter—but if your hours vanish into random scrolling and last-minute cramming, your calendar tells a different story. Wisdom counts days, not to stress you out, but to help you live on purpose.

Start with the "big rocks"—the most important things—then fit the rest around them:

- » God: Bible, prayer, church.
- » School: classes, homework blocks.
- » Health: sleep, movement, meals.
- » Relationships: family time, friends.
- » Extras: sports, work, hobbies.

Use time blocks. Plan your week on Sunday night. Set study sprints (25 minutes focus, 5 minutes break). Put your phone in another room when you work. Protect a small Sabbath window each week for rest and worship (yes, even students need this). Say yes to what aligns with your calling—and no to what steals it.

Expect interruptions, but don't live in them. When you slip, reset the next block instead of quitting the day. Over time, your schedule will look more like who you want to become.

Numbering your days reminds you they're gifts. Spend them like they matter—because they do.

A Prayer for You

Lord, teach me to value my time and use it wisely. Help me plan with purpose, focus when it's time to work, and rest when it's time to stop. Order my steps this week. Amen.

Your Challenge

Make a one-week time map. Block your school, sleep, workouts, and a daily 15-minute God-time. Add two study sprints per weekday. Review next Sunday: what worked, what didn't, and one change to make.

Take a Moment

» Where do my hours leak?

» One "big rock" I'll schedule first:

» One thing I will say "no" to this week:

Week 52: Run Your Race—Finish Strong

"Therefore, since we are surrounded by so great a cloud of witnesses, let us also lay aside every weight, and sin which clings so closely, and let us run with endurance the race that is set before us, looking to Jesus..." — Hebrews 12:1-2 (ESV)

Devotional Thought

You've made it to Week 52. But this isn't the finish line—it's a checkpoint. Life with Jesus is a long race, not a quick sprint. Hebrews tells us how to run: drop the weights, ditch the sin, and keep your eyes on Jesus.

Weights aren't always bad things; they're anything that slows you down: wasted time, unhealthy comparisons, habits that drain you. Sin tangles your feet. Confess it. Throw it off. Then run light. Endurance is built in ordinary days—stacked choices, faithful habits, small obediences that add up to a strong life.

You're not running alone. Others have gone before you—family, pastors, mentors, faithful believers through the centuries. Their stories cheer you on. And Jesus is not just the finish line—He's your pace-setter and your strength. He endured the cross for you. He knows how to carry you through hard miles.

Look back with gratitude: Where did you grow this year? Where did God meet you? Look ahead with courage: What race is set before you now—school, family, friendships, faith? Lift your eyes. Keep moving. One step at a time.

A Prayer for You

Jesus, thank You for bringing me this far. Help me lay aside every weight and sin. Give me endurance to run my race, eyes fixed on You. Use my life for Your glory and others' good. Amen.

Your Challenge

Choose three practices from this year to carry forward (e.g., morning time with God, weekly church + serving, accountability for purity). Write a letter to your future self (6 months from now) about the man you're becoming and the steps you'll take. Set a reminder to read it.

Take a Moment

» One weight I need to lay aside:

» One sin I need to confess:

» Three practices I'm keeping:

Discover More Books

Start each day with purpose, peace, and spiritual renewal.

Whether you're guiding teens in faith or growing closer as a family—this devotional series meets you right where you are.

Collect the Whole Series

Devotional for
Parents and Kids

Devotional for
Teen Girls

Devotional for
Teen Boys

Available at major online bookstores

Each book is a spiritual companion. Together, they form a complete journey—personal, relational, and transformative.

Don't wait—bring home the full devotional set and let every day draw you closer to faith, love, and lasting renewal.

www.ingramcontent.com/pod-product-compliance
Lightning Source LLC
Chambersburg PA
CBHW031438120626
46545CB00006B/2463